CW00447478

A Respectable
Neighbourhood
Sue Boyle

Sue Boyle

A RESPECTABLE
NEIGHBOURHOOD

Time & Tide Publishing
London EC1

Published by Time & Tide Publishing 2013
London ECI

COVER
A street in the Guidecca

ISBN-13: 978-1490946917

A CIP catalogue record for this book
is available from the British Library.

timeandtidepublishing@gmail.com

contents

ONE

TWO

THREE

Prologue

They all gave place when the signing was done, and Little Dorrit and her husband walked out of the church alone. They paused for a moment on the steps of the portico, looking at the fresh perspective of the street in the autumn morning sun's bright rays, and then went down.

Went down into a modest life of usefulness and happiness. Went down to give a mother's care, in the fulness of time, to Fanny's neglected children, no less than to their own, and to leave that lady going into Society for ever and a day. Went down to give a tender nurse and friend to Tip for some few years, who was never vexed by the great exactions he made of her, in return for the riches he might have given her if he had ever had them, and who lovingly closed his eyes upon the Marshalsea and all its blighted fruits. They went quietly down into the roaring streets, inseparable and blessed; and as they passed along in sunshine and shade, the noisy and the eager, and the arrogant and the froward and the vain, fretted and chafed, and made their usual uproar.

Charles Dickens

Little Dorrit
First published by Bradbury & Evans
Lombard Street, London 1855-1857

ONE

a respectable
neighbourhood

Our neighbour the lady
puts on airs. My brother says
she steals Gurney's grey horse
from the stables at midnight
and rides down the High Street
naked. White as moonlight,
stark white as the moonlight
at midnight, my brother says.

pavarotti
at the grosvenor house hotel

He ate like one whose happiness is food.
The juice of Thracian pomegranates; bread,
proved overnight and set to bake at dawn;
cheese, apples, a dish of raisins, eggs –
his eyes shone with delight. He was the feast
in every particle, as on stage that night
he would be the music, the music utterly,
and later, she knew, in his bed he would be love.

It was the god in him, to be what he did –
it was his genius. At Wembley, a whole city
would pay to hear him sing. She watched him eat
and knew that he was the fire at the heart
of life. He cut the comb, spread it, oozing honey,
on warm bread and asked her name.

Eurydice, she said.

a leisure centre
is also a temple of learning

The honey-coloured girl in the women's changing room
is absorbed in making her body more beautiful:
she has flexed and toned every muscle with a morning swim
and showered away the pool chemicals
using an aromatic scrub and a gentle exfoliant.

She has perfect bone structure: her secret cleft
is shaved as neatly as a charlatan's moustache.
In dreamy abstractedness she moisturises
then spray perfumes every part that might be loved –
tipped throat, underchin, the little kisspoints
below her ears, the nuzzle between her breasts,
her willow thighs.

A bee could sip her.

She is summer cream slipped over raspberries

and so much younger than the rest of us.

She should look around.

We twelve are the chorus:

we know what happens next.

mr marksbury's
careful choice of beds

From the Camden Town house clearance specialists,
with their stuffed birds, hallstands, cracked majolica
and out of tune pianos −

from the flotsam and jetsam of other shipwrecked lives
following her divorce, my great aunt Irene
furnished her two rooms.

After he closed the shop for the evening,
Mr Marksbury would deliver her purchases,
take a glass of port and reminisce

about those days when totters
could harvest London with a horse and cart
and the pickings if you were sharp −

a nice bit of cranberry, in the better streets
an unchipped piece of genuine Lalique −
but would not cross the hall into Irene's bedroom

though he himself had supplied the figured walnut bed
because that would have been a sure way in his opinion
to lose an extremely good customer.

A shame he would say quite often to his partner, Mr Paul
that our friend on the hill has never remarried.
She has an eye for a pretty thing.

the happiness
of mr paul

We like Mr Marksbury's shop.
The carved bear hallstand
Johannes Brahms is not for sale
nor the wax death mask
of the third Napoleon.

Mr Marksbury's aunt and uncle
were a Pearly King and Queen
with a lock-up in Whitechapel
and a horse, Madison,
who pulled the cart.
Their godson Cyril was made
up on his twenty-first birthday
to a Pearly Prince.

On Sunday evenings Mr Paul
opens one of the parlour pianos
and rehearses our club routines.
At nine o'clock precisely
Mr Marksbury brings Earl Grey tea.

Mr Paul's mother
launched him when he was five.
His costume was sailor suits
with colour coded ribbons on the hats –
pink for the cheeky songs,
blue for the weepies.
For Whitechapel weddings,
he was always in demand.

Mr Paul has not played in public
since he moved in with Mr Marksbury.
I've hung up my pumps, he says.
You don't put yourself out for money
when you've found true love.

seize the day
or words to that effect

Why procrastinate, I said to him? What do we stand to gain if we delay? We might have been bashful, signed up together for a Path to True Happiness twelve week evening course, or treated ourselves to a Nile cruise to consult the sphinx. I can just see us on the foredeck in the evening, each of us brooding separately about the peril of commitment after so many years of living on his own.

But the body clocks were ticking. I was not exactly in the first flush when I fell in with Mr Paul and given our beliefs we could hardly expect a second bite of the cherry on the other side. Besides, I'm a businessman. My accountant was bound to say that living in two places was not an allowable expense. We were men of the world. After a couple of weeks, there seemed no point in it.

So I said, Mr Paul, why don't we just quit the dithering and get one of those partnerships? We'll be quids in on taxi fares if we tie the knot and we'll also be able to raise some extra stock capital on your flat. And he said, those are my sentiments exactly, Mr M, I'm glad you spoke up. *Carpe diem*, or words to that effect.

Grab your opportunities this side of the pearlies is our view. You never know what's going to happen next.

ezra jackson
and the cat lady

Might I have married her?
The cats were comfortable with me.
I liked her house.

I used to go up to dig the burials
lay each corpse on its bed of straw
and plant a rose.

The first time – so much blossom in the wind
the grass and her dark hair were starred with it
the earth was easy, that warm moist of spring

but in dead winter, cracking it with a pick
for Old Max One-Eye, Max the Molecatcher –
where did she get such names?

Tabitha Lily, Pantomimus,
Little Bobbins, Empress Valentine –
I asked her if she took them out of books.

Cats bring their names when they come to you, she said,
and take them to their next life when they go.

I liked the way the fields butted her hedge;
summer, the windsounds in the waves of wheat;
the larks' shrill descant all the long day long
above the deep churr of Gurney's harvester.
She told me the cats competed for her bed.

Boris the Terrible, my gorgeous boy
with that wicked growl on him. He gets there first,
but some cold nights I sleep with all fourteen.

trust your instincts
not your baedeker

The way to find yourself is lose the path,
a poet said who went this way before.
In Venice, to reach the seaborn city's heart,
the straight way is the worst. You should ignore

(the poet said who went this way before)
in Venice, as in love, the offered chart.
The straight way is the worst. You should ignore
the sign that points you 'This way to St Marks.'

In Venice, as in love, disdain the chart:
the best way is to choose the unnumbered door.
The sign that points you 'This way to St Marks'
distracts you from the gap in the cloister wall.

The best way is to choose the unnumbered door,
the shutter's negligence, the gate unbarred,
the unrecorded gap in the cloister wall.
In seizing the unexpected lies the art −

the shutter's negligence, the gate unbarred−
in Venice, to reach the seaborn city's heart,
in seizing the unexpected lies the art.
The way to find yourself is lose the path.

the place called argentina

Her book says Julius Caesar was murdered here,
where the tramlines end. There are beggars,
police in their *blindati*, foreign priests.
The lovers are new to each other.
It will be their first night in Rome.

Caesar was slaughtered in Pompey's curia
in daylight, by his friends, for the good of Rome.
She will learn to say *buon giorno, per favore*
and gasp 'Alessandro' when he makes love to her.
She imagines this love will last.

These pine trees burrow ancient temple floors
to nurture themselves in older, unhallowed earth.
There are warnings to tourists in five languages.
Do not pet the cats. They respond to affection.
They will follow you into the traffic and will die.

There were temples here to the gods and goddesses
of fountains, fertility, the safe passage of sailors,
the good luck of the current day. Now starlings
funnel their black murmurations
in among the pines and disappear.

She imagines the folding of ten thousand wings.
L'amore. La morte. How close they are.
The confusion of signs. The fiction of surfaces.

TWO

imaginary prisons

Below the graceful lie the graceless truths –
dungeons, tunnels, gargoyles, gaolers, chains,
stairways to nowhere,
thumbscrews, turning wheels,
broken bridges across the void.

But how lovely the surface is –

setts rinsed by rain now, polished by winter sun,
fountains playing, flowers on the stalls,
these pavement exiles making the day weep
with their accordions, voices, violins, guitars.

So for a season

enraptured by the glory of the flesh
lovers forget their hidden histories
but lines are already bitten in the plate.
Lift the inked paper from the press
dear creatures. Your truths will out.

The Carceri etchings
Giovanni Piranesi, Rome 1750

dolls
at the newark fair

The under-age Irish girls
in arm-linked cohorts flaunt around the fair –
cheeky, short-skirted, high-heeled, painted up,
flowers and fancy combs in their long thick hair.

By gaslight in palatial caravans
their fathers, uncles, brothers split the take
and oversee their sisters', daughters',
nieces' virgin sleep.

In the night pavilions, dolls,
with their halcyon absence of genitalia,
wait for the dawn collectors.
Strong men patrol the fierce perimeter.

the death
of eurydice

To bring in the dark notes,
that was why it went the way it did.
To balance the beauty
so that his music and all the music
that came after him
would ring true.

Now Orpheus could sing
the house of cards,
the great ship going down,
the spread of the cancer,
the failure to love the wren,
the snake in the grass,
the young bride's requiem.

the mother
of the bride

Easy too easy in her narrow bed
she dreams a green garden, dew on dancing feet.
By this day's fail, by fall of this day's night
my dreaming daughter will become a wife.

We braid her hair to take the cobweb veil;
a milk-white gown
flowers and floats and flows about her now;
my daughter has become a peerless bride.

Father, priest, husband, black as cormorants,
before the high altar will transact her price –
how thin this band of gold, how much too slight
to sell this daughter, to acquire this wife.

Then she must take the heady wedding wine;
reach the cold knife to cut the offered cake;
pierce the deceptive ice white shell and find
the dark midwinter of her married life.

the wedding
in the strand

They could be lapdancers.
They could be goddesses
waiting in line for the photographer
outside St Clement Danes.
Slender, startling and immaculate
in crepe de Chine with boned
and sculptured sweetheart bodices
and Giuseppe Zanotti sandals
with crystal anklestraps.
They have come to support the bride.

On the Thames river boat Arcadia,
the wedding party has booked
the full silver service –
goats cheese panacotta, chargrilled
fillet of salmon, summer pudding
and pink champagne.

Late afternoon –
palaces glide past and penthouses,
monuments and temples to absent gods.
The familiar city is disappearing.
The western river resembles
a roadway of shining fire.

Our bride folds herself like a fan
against the flank of her new husband
and twists the lovely ring.
She is nineteen.
Her big day is ending.
Suddenly she is afraid.

to forget
her unfaithful husband

my sister flies to a country
where ancient forests are on fire
and creatures are their own
charred hieroglyphs.
Birds are black bones.
Lizards have shrivelled
in their blistered skins.

Fire spits in Athens
and Arcadia.
It frightens Pelion.
Ash coats the surface
of the mourning sea.
Who among us
can promise a greenshoot spring?

This is where I belong, says my sister.
I too am a relic of myself.
The husband I loved did this.
He laid waste my lovely world.

crossing
the lagoon

After the gasp, the jostle
and the fractured palaces
afloat on their own
dream images like swans,
on the Piazza St Marco
at the masquerade
a firebird touched
her shoulder with its wing.

Her husband said
Venice was overcrowded
and overpriced.
They would not come back.

Years afterwards in his bed
she swims windows
reflected in water,
shedding her exile,
single, glinting,
lissome as a fish.

alone

on living's hard shoulder
the one with all the voices in his head

while nuclear families stream
to their distant seductive places
with carloads of children, bravado,
iPods, waterwings

marooned at life's starting place
dumbfounded spectator
of hectic and unspooling
generations

his name going nowhere

joyrider

notice him

heat

After Sheila was stabbed our street was quieter

but her empty house made everyone afraid.
We were afraid what unfamiliar anger
might move in. We were afraid of fire.

Scorched parks, wide-open windows, casual lust.
Hot babies bawled in kitchens, women snapped,
men and children always underfoot.

Sheila was stabbed with the knife she carried
to protect herself. In Mile End Hospital
three days and nights she was too ill to give her name.

Forgotten three days and nights, her dogs went mad –
the alsatians, the puppies whimpering behind the door,
waterless, no comforting, no food.

Police called a locksmith to slip the yale
and wardens who fetched the creatures one by one,
leashed, but compliant, unwary

as if they knew their rescuers meant no harm.
It was August Bank Holiday. The pound was already full.
The sergeant said they would have to put them down.

lost girl

A Harlot's Progress Plate I
William Hogarth

She was a greedy suckling, sir, not the timid thing you've painted her at all. Such mouth on her. Her eyes were ravenous. As a parched throat will have water and the salmon get to the sea, that was my daughter, sir. Your city was in her blood. She ravened for what you had.

Perhaps it was my fault, sir. I knew I was carrying a daughter and I used to say, Life will be good to you my girl. Your mother will see to that. Meaning that I would love her and care for her, sir, and find her a good husband, a better one than mine. But my daughter didn't want tenderness, nor the kind of life her mother understood. I knew I'd lose her to the city. I knew it even though I didn't have the wit myself to know what a city was.

You've drawn her so exactly, sir – those downcast eyes, that bonnet tilted so you wanted to get up close to see more of her pretty face. I dressed that bonnet, sir. I put those ribbons on. Look at the scissors and pincushion hung from her waist as if to say she looked for nothing better in London than seamstress work – it was all a show, sir. The shyness, the nice handkerchief across her bosom, the dainty stepping down into the dirt. Everyone who sees your picture knows the truth about my daughter – what she is, the pleasure to be had from her, the money to be made.

A hawk, sir – his claws are as sharp as rapiers, but when he picks the leveret from the field, it can seem at first that he means no harm. There won't be a mark on the poor creature at the first, nor a puncture in the tender skin. It's only later he rips her, starting at the throat.

She was an ignorant, yearning creature, sir, hungry for everything she couldn't have. A gentleman like you with such a power to look down on the rest of us – who else could have warned my daughter when she stepped down from that conveyance – who else, unless you, Mr Hogarth, who must have been standing by?

christmas market

In this theatre of soft toy tigers,
Bernini fountains, parachute Santas
and festive trivia,
in front of the Sicilian nougat stand
another woman's daughter
with a fishbowl of clear water on her head
performs for the cameras
of the Christmas crowd.

In stillness, soft white gloves
and embroidered petticoats,
she takes tribute from Chicago,
Tokyo, Perth and Huddersfield.
Snow flurries dust the cobbles and are gone.

If they see her tomorrow selecting aubergines,
browsing a bookstand, praying at the crib
or flashing her eyes in a midnight street at men,
if she shows them even six pomegranate seeds
as proof that she has returned to them
from the dark,
even then they might not know her,
any more than I might know you,
if I found you here, restored
after such a time –

Eurydice, my wife.

Persephone, my daughter.

Piazza Navona, Rome

persephone

I do not mourn you, mother,
there, nor want this day,
this dazzle, hills wide open,
footpaths through hot fields,
these hours without
the sweet dark heft of him.

I am not your daughter there
but the root of things,
their speechless origin
and he their silent end.

Reluctant I walk your earth
for its wakeful season.
I am thralled to winter now
and so cold
it will break your heart.

dinner
at the regents park hotel

Skilled and tenacious with her fillet steak,
its lard of foie gras, its mousseline
of crushed redcurrant moistened
with cointreau, she plays her tonguetip slyly
along her lips and sips her little wine.
The bachelor reads correctly
the cunning twists of gold at her ears,
her wrists and round her pulsing throat
as signs that she is ready for a mate.

The bachelor is a herpetologist.
Reticulated python in London Zoo
follow his fingers' movement on their glass
with fixity that has the look of love,
but in the wild, as he knows all too well,
can throw one strangling coil and gulp
(shoulders, belly, struggling haunches, hooves)
an antelope headfirst.

the married woman
speaks

Father used to say, sooner I can get you out of school and off my hands, Marie girl, the happier I shall be, if anyone will have you, so spruce yourself up a bit. But take my word – book learning's not attractive to a man. Learn to make the best of what you've got.

So I took Father at his word and got Albert Hawkins to marry me – poor Albert Hawkins, with his regulation haircut and his nice new uniform. We went down the registry and I brought him back to Hammersmith for tea and I told Father that Albert would be sleeping in my bed from now on seeing as we were man and wife, and we would take our tea in the parlour, not the back kitchen, thank you, seeing as it was our wedding day.

Then I said, my husband and I are going to promenade now, Father, down the Mall, and we'll take our supper in the Black Lion and then come home to bed. Don't wait up for us. I'm a married woman now, Father, I used to say, and you'll mind your tongue please when you speak to me. And I'll take a whisky, thank you, with a little water, not too much.

Bert didn't like to see me drink. When he was overseas, I'd go out with his friend Jack Bannister who was in a reserved occupation and had a nice polished way with him. We'd go up West and sometimes take in a show. You're smart as paint Marie, Jack used to say, smart as bloomin' paint. A right little handful. And you can hold your drink. I'm glad you're not my wife.

colours

My grandmother Lily was born the year
the Whitechapel murder victims died.
She filled her garden with flowers –
fuschias, geraniums, african marigolds –
anything for some colour. One year
she painted the iron railings,
the wicker chairs, the window frames
and the garden bench pale pink.
Another year the paint was all blood red.
Every night, in her dreams, her second boy
John fell down the sky in flames.
Five sisters wore white at her wedding.
Lily told me the wrong things are what lasts.

the life of the bee
by maurice maeterlinck

This was my great aunt's book –
Rose, the Baptist schoolteacher
who loved her diminutive pupils –
the girls in their serviceable cotton pinafores,
the boys in their awkward boots –
and also loved her friend Frances
another churchgoing spinster schoolteacher
but offered no one the key
to the hidden door of her honey-chambered self
and like her friend Frances
never suffered the invasion of a man –

neither the glory nor the disgrace of it.

the road
to appleby

My friend said the Horse Fair
will mend your heart so I took the bus

through Temple Sowerby
and Crackenthorpe

with my heart's hurting pieces,
with my grieving womb

and I saw girls in Appleby like eels, like otters
rough tough healthy boys, people like acrobats

on each other's shoulders, up up up
the more and the further generations

the strongest rock solid
the weakest and the topmost unafraid.

I saw horses unsaddled unbridled
unconstrained in the rush and canter
of the river's cold clean water

and no one looked my way,
not one reached out to me.

Childless in that exultation of creatures –
what comfort could come from that?

too late
for the love hotel

Only the louche and lovely can rent these rooms
where Balkan girls drowse in their bankers' arms
and boys dispose lean limbs to delight their friends.

Little Mozart lodged down this street;
here Beethoven's pupils climbed four flights to reach
their suffering great man. The bombs

which rubbled the virtuous houses left intact
the Orient Hotel, which now with such a show
of tenderness refuses us a room.

We join Middle Europe in the Palmenhaus
where an Emperor used to watch his butterflies
fold and fan their gaudy painted wings –

dry creatures in sight of a garden,
coffee with pastries, a palace of dusty glass.

Tiefer Graben, Vienna

waiting for a king
in ithaca

The dog we called Argus
drowsed all day by the door
of the black barn. At intervals a frog
would startle the pond or the drowsing cat
would stretch its forepaws, yawn
and revert to indolence.

There were larks in the high dry air.
My mother used to weep
in her upstairs room
and even in summer keep
split logs and brittle twigs in the hearth
for the king's return.

There were ice rings every winter
round the moon. We heard of ships
turned suddenly to stone
by an angry god or spiralled down
a whirlpool's roaring throat
and of a king and his sailors flung
on a wall of milk green water,
broken like matchwood,
howling at the sun.

dido's
lament

My story's simply told. I was the Queen
of fabled Carthage. Nothing now remains
but my sad song. Who would remember me

unless Aeneas, sheltering from the sea,
had charmed me from myself with his strange tales?
My story's simply told. I was the Queen

fierce in my widowhood and chastity
ambushed by sudden love and then betrayed.
Without my song, who would remember me?

My horses, ships all gone, the great city
I raised from barren sand. No thing remains.
My story's simply told. I was the Queen.

No man in Carthage would have dared to speak
to me of love. A handsome stranger came.
Without my song, who would remember me

and my sad life? It was my fate to be
both pitied and reviled. Love turned to shame.
My story's simply told. I was the Queen.
Without my song, who would remember me?

THREE

views from the bridge

one
The Canada goose rasps on the river embankment
like a blunt ripsaw fighting through green wood.
This is a wild creature who has lost its mate.

Every morning we pass and we do not speak of it.
One day one of us will wish
we had the brass neck to noise off like this.

two
I did not go to that place to bring you home
but to leave you in for the long stay.
I am not Orpheus. I cannot sing.

Dark sticks to me now like oil to a guillemot.
The boatman smiled.
He will know me when I come again.

three
The way this river cannot be divided
but circumvents what tries to hinder it
and remains one thing.

The way an ocean is always just one water –
a blade cannot sever it nor can you break it
with any blow.

So it seemed to me when I had your love.

the statue of antinous

This is the legend of the young man Antinous
who after a night with his lover the emperor,
his limbs still heavy with the ache of loving
and being loved,
his mouth lax with their kissing
and the emperor's yearning still like salt
on his lovely skin

walked from the summer palace into the Nile,
the water embracing him, the light breeze
lifting and ruffling his hair
as so often the emperor's fingers had ruffled it

walked and went on walking
until his footing disappeared from under him
and still drowsy he went below the waves

where he remained,
cherished by the river nineteen centuries,
until three enraptured archaeologists,
marvelling at the glossy pallor of his skin,
declared him always to have been a statue
and gave the world a completely different
account of his story,

never themselves having feared
(as Antinous the beautiful must have feared)
that they might grow old and unlovable,

who had never themselves been asked
to live out their years
the forsaken favourite of an emperor.

the war wife's almanac

In January she prepared her house for a homecoming –
rosemary, bergamot, thyme in every room.

In February she knew that her belly contained the world.

In March she asked her father to make a cot.

In April the cousins in Back Street
received their telegrams.

In May she looked for comfort among the cows –
the dairy smelt of urine, milk and dung. It smelt of hay.

In June Charlie Sladbrook came home without his legs.

In July she dreamt that the earth would lose the moon.

In August she and her mother bottled greengages.

In September she howled her heart out
and named her son Jack after his grandfather.

In October she learnt to say the word Passchendaele.

In November the troop trains kept going south.
She refused to pray for the welfare of the king.

In December she said, I have a son.
I am a person who does not give in to grief.

the sailor's wife

That man's a bit of rough, her neighbours said,
the way he swaggers back to her waiting bed,
the mess he makes of her cleanly home,
his cunning eye.
He sailed into the silence of the snow.
In the space between two breaths, his doctor said,
as a ship can slip its mooring ropes too soon
on a too high tide, any heart can fail.
She kept his compass on her windowsill,
his boots and walkstick by her garden door
and refused to mourn. A widow is still a wife,
she used to say. I am not alone.
To fall from view is not the same as lost.
To journey a different sea is not the same as gone.

another day

lemons like round bright lamps will gleam
still in their glossy mantle of winter leaves.
The weather contraption will still register
each shift of wind, each change of temperature.
The pond between the clumps of Canary palms
will have this same lazy traffic of golden carp
and ring-necked parakeets
will be swooping and screeching among the trees
the same,
but the painted bench
there, by the steps up to the fountain,
where he is reading *La Stampa* now in the winter sun
will be empty. He will have gone.
And I will be the woman who was loved.

the evensong

I will not be long away
I told him at the gate,
but it pleased me too much,
the road, the afternoon,
my strong new bicycle.

*My lover warmed me more
than my husband's hearth.*

It pleased me too much
to let the bell toll on,
the road too long
the day too short
to go back home.

*Husband and lover
were my world.*

Now they are gone,
but the same bell tolls
the evensong each day
and when I kneel to pray
for their two souls
it pleases me
how light still reaches in
from the west
to warm the stone.

I am growing old.

To my lover
I say in my prayers,
wait, I will not be long,
and to the other,
my husband, I whisper,
I will come home soon.
I have been too long gone.

the afterword

For the first time ever, the poets laureate were unanimous. On major issues their usual habit was to wrangle and squabble themselves into public exhaustion and then demand an arbiter, but on this they were adamant. The poem sealed in the plain lead casket was the only possible piece to include in the 'Our Greatest Achievements' time capsule the world was sending towards the unknown but so much hoped for star. The laureates refused either to identify the poem or to publish it. How would any poet in the future dare to put metaphorical pen to metaphorical paper if he knew that ultimate beauty had already been achieved? The secret must die with us, they insisted. And die with them it did.

In real time, the story must end here. The little capsule was launched successfully and disappeared into the unimaginable reaches of deep space. Earth had been devoured by its flaming parent many million years before the answer came. Fortunately, the old conventions of terrestrial narrative allow us to find out what it said.

Dear Friends. Your travelling collection of ingenious but essentially worthless artefacts taught us so much about what it is for a civilisation to lose its path. We were greatly touched by them. The one word sent by your poets, however, proved a truly inspiring gift. With this word, 'love', for many generations every poet on our planet has had enough material to compose his lifetime of poems and lyric song. We also came to appreciate your wisdom in sending just one word for in this way you shared with us the deep truth that the most perfectly beautiful poem is always the one where the most is left unsaid. You are ghosts now, wandering the great mysteries of interstellar space. To comfort you, in this golden casket we reciprocate your gift. As you yourselves taught us, one word, if it is the right word, is enough.

the magician's wife

one

He was the best of husbands. At our wedding
The church was almost full.
Mr Cupid had his friend Mr Albert as best man –
matching costumes of lavender silk twill,
pearl buttons, ribbon bindings, white kid shoes.

They did a double act, to produce the ring –
Mr Albert pretending he had forgotten it,
Mr Cupid pretending to be annoyed with him,
all in mime. You have to be respectful in a church.
Then Mr Cupid did one of his scarf tricks
and after a lot of clever business
produced the ring from Mr Albert's ear.
Everyone clapped except the vicar –
I think he was a bit surprised.

They did the photographs outside the church.
Mr Cupid told me when to toss the bouquet –
Throw it really high girl, he whispered,
high up as you can.
And it went so high, of course, that it disappeared
which was what they'd planned.
While everyone was staring up at the empty sky
Mr Cupid was able to slip away unnoticed –
he had an engagement that night in Manchester.

Then Mr Albert clapped his hands
and white rose petals started falling,
enough for everyone, falling softly, falling very slow,
what Japanese magicians sometimes call
'Sky Filled With Summer Snow.'

Everyone agreed it was a beautiful wedding.
Later they changed the faces in the photographs
to make it seem that Mr Cupid had been there all along.
It's a wonder, the new technology.

two
I never saw his rooms. I never asked.
In summer he had engagements by the sea.
He'd find me somewhere really nice to stay
and meet me every night after the show –
those were our best times.

One night he took me down to the sands
all ribbed and cockled where the tide had been.
The sea was silver in the moonlight;
the air was very clear
and he showed me a boat crossing the bay.
It had an owl and a cat in it, still as obelisks,
sitting bolt upright, staring at the moon.
Their eyes were glittering.

Mr Cupid said, look, they are going to be married,
and I said, they'll be happy
for ever after then, just like us,
and he said 'yes' and walked me home.

I didn't see him again.
But I have no complaints.
It was a wonderful marriage.
I have had my enchanted life.

mr marksbury's advice

If you are lucky in this life, Ada,
and continue to be a considerate
and sensitive young girl,
one day one of the few remaining angels
might materialise for a moment,
retract his astonishing white wings
and ask you to help him voice
the terrible yearning for human affection
which assails his heart.

You will long to respond
but being a lonely and emotionally
a rather neglected young person
and shackled perhaps also
by what Mr Paul and I regard
as your over-strict upbringing
you might be too timorous –
the affectionate word might stay
unuttered inside your mouth.

It might then be your sorrow
to watch your unique opportunity
to experience love fly on.
Outcomes in this life are so often
less kindly than your average fairytale
would have you think.
I have been fortunate in love.
Be courageous, said Mr Marksbury.

postscript

morning discovers
veils and cool white dresses
brides have been chosen
light lifts from the glassy rivers
like a song

Acknowledgements

I am very grateful to the editors of *Acumen, Magma, Poetry Ireland Review* and *The Rialto* in which several of these poems first appeared and to Smith/Doorstop for publishing others in *Too Late for the Love Hotel* which was one of the prize-winners in *The North*'s 2010 pamphlet competition judged by the Poet Laureate Andrew Motion.

'A Leisure Centre is Also a Temple of Learning' was first published in *The Rialto* and then in the *Forward Book of Poetry 2010*. Subsequently it was selected for the Forward *Poems of the Decade* which was published in 2012. It was also featured by the Welsh singer/songwriter/author/broadcaster Cerys Matthews as the final item in her BBC Radio 4 programme *With Great Pleasure* in July 2012.

In 2009, 'The Magician's Wife' won the Evelyn Sandford Senior Literary Trophy in the Creative Writing Section in the Mid Somerset Festival. In the same year 'The Road to Appleby' won Second Prize in the Wells Festival of Literature poetry competition.

Sue Boyle

L'amore. *La morte*. How close they are.
The confusion of signs. The fiction of surfaces.

Sue Boyle's *Too Late for the Love Hotel* was a prizewinner in *The North*'s 2010 pamphlet competition judged by the Poet Laureate Sir Andrew Motion who said that the collection stood out for 'the attention the poems pay to their subjects' and 'the range and strangeness of its interests.' In *On Board Arcadia* the lover of the Emperor Hadrian tells his story alongside the piano-playing partner of a Camden Town house clearance dealer; Cosimo Duke of Tuscany shares space with Henri Rousseau's talking cat. An eighteenth century mother grieves for her ruined daughter to William Hogarth while the goddess Demeter looks for her own lost daughter in a Christmas Market in contemporary Rome.

Sue Boyle likes her characters to step out of history, darkness and silence and confide the core truths about their lives without the author getting in the way. Trained to teach drama and creative writing, she writes direct and accessible poems for the voice – or rather for the many voices in the series of short volumes which make up *On Board Arcadia*. A Londoner by family and background, she has lived in ten English counties and worked as a teacher, social worker, antiquarian print dealer, market trader in bric-a-brac and maker of hand-finished picture frames. For the past six years she has organised the Bath Poetry Cafe and the associated Cafe Writing Days.

Arcadia is a world full of surprise and revelation as the poems explore what lies below the surface of the ordinary and bring old histories into the present day. 'Sue Boyle's is the voice of a true original: her work has a wit and inventiveness all too rare in poetry today.' (Rosie Bailey)

On Board Arcadia

*A series of six themed short volumes
available at readings and workshops
or direct from Amazon.*

Volume One
A Day Out on the Thames
Twenty-two poems

Against a background of momentous historical events – the fires of the London blitz, the dropping of the atom bomb, the terrors of the Cold War – the poems in *A Day Out on the Thames* focus their affectionate attention on the aspirations and disappointments of one London family: the texture of treasured moments, daily life and familiar places, the complex of memories which becomes the inheritance of those who are left behind. There are sorrows, difficulty, loneliness, and loss, but it is the passion for living and for the wonder of life which the poems celebrate. The collection closes with the serenity of the prize-winning sonnet, 'Thinking About the Swans.'

October 2013
ISBN-13:978-1483961668

Volume Two
Mr Marksbury's Careful Choice of Beds
Twenty-two poems

Mr Marksbury's Careful Choice of Beds is a book about London, but not perhaps the London the tourist knows. One by one, strange characters make their intriguing cameo appearances: Virgil Christopher the living statue; Flavia the poledancer; the lonely collector of vintage glass. We visit a country auction and overnight at a giant antiques fair. We also meet a rescue ferret, a unicorn, a couple of angels and a famous talking cat. From Kew Gardens to Canary Wharf, Camden Town antiques dealer Mr Marksbury makes his way through this offbeat geography, shedding light on dark places and offering his idiosyncratic views on leading the good life. There are also useful lessons on how to fake an old master painting, lie down safely with a lion and recognise true love.

October 2013
ISBN-13:978-1491021880

Volume Three
A Respectable Neighbourhood
Thirty-nine poems

Behind the closed doors of houses, the closed doors of the heart – the secrets, dangers, delights and sorrows of human love. From first encounters to bereavement, with lovers ranging back from the contemporary to the depths of ancient myth, the collection takes its theme from 'A Leisure Centre is Also a Temple of Learning' and explores 'what happens next.' Will we be faithful, unfaithful, cherished, abandoned, blameworthy, innocent? We never know what waits behind the door until we make the frightening commitment to step inside the house of love.

October 2013
ISBN-13: 978-1490946917

Volume Four
Report from the Judenplatz
Nine Lamentations & A Play for Witnesses

The sequence of nine lamentations in *Report from the Judenplatz* is also presented as a play for witnesses to be shared by any number of participants as a way of honouring the victims of the Holocaust. Between 1939 and 1945 most of Europe turned its back on its Jewish citizens. This book tries to hear the voice of those absences – the abiding silence of the streets and squares emptied by the deportations – and to make a space in which to remember the richness of the culture which the Nazi genocide intended to destroy. The cover design is by kind permission of the Yad Vashem Holocaust Memorial and Institute in Jerusalem and profits from the sale of *Report from the Judenplatz* will be donated to the Yad Vashem UK Foundation.

October 2013
ISBN-13:978-1482776294

Volume Five
Ark Music
Twenty-six poems

Ark Music, the fifth volume of *On Board Arcadia*, is a strange, dark collection which explores the belief that man is the intended master of the earth. From the first lobe-finned fish to the last extinction, from the Trojan War to the threat of nuclear armageddon, we are casualties of our species' ambition and belligerence. A grieving celebration of the wonder and beauty of the planet as it turns in its 'cage of stars', the poems in *Ark Music* reach towards a gentler way of being in the world and try to open up a place in imagination for a new 'ark' so that what is left of the precious, varied and fragile might be better cherished and perhaps be saved.

October 2013
ISBN-13:978-1491041772

coming soon

Volume Six
A Small Menagerie

Time & Tide Publishing
London EC1

Made in the USA
Charleston, SC
08 October 2013